FINALLY WAKING UP

Living your Best Life Now! Getting Sober, Healthy and Losing Weight

John Epifanio

Copyright © 2022 John Epifanio

All rights reserved

The characters and events portrayed in this book are fictitious. Any similarity to real persons, living or dead, is coincidental and not intended by the author.

No part of this book may be reproduced, or stored in a retrieval system, or transmitted in any form or by any means, electronic, mechanical, photocopying, recording, or otherwise, without express written permission of the publisher.

ISBN-13: 978-1-959555-01-8
ISBN-10:

Cover design by: John Epifanio
Library of Congress Control Number: 2018675309
Printed in the United States of America

This book is dedicated to my father Jack Epifanio- a great man who put the well being of his family and friends above everything else. He took his life by his own hand while in the clutches of alcohol addiction. So that his death (and the tortured existence leading up to that day) not be in vain, I seek to help others to achieve a peaceful existence in sobriety.

"God, grant me the serenity to accept the things I cannot change, courage to change the things I can, and wisdom to know the difference"

SERENITY PRAYER

FINALLY WAKING UP

Living your Best Life Now! Getting Sober, Healthy and Losing Weight

By John Epifanio

TABLE OF CONTENTS:

PART 1 - My History and Relationship with Alcohol

My Early Life

The First Time

High School

College and the Marijuana Years

All Grown Up, Drinking for Fun and "Crossing the Line"

Hitting Close to Home - Losing Loved Ones to Drinking

PART 2-The Problem: Quitting

and Moderation Attempts

The Problems Brought on by Drinking

I Got This Now, I Can Have Just One

My Failed Moderation Attempts

The Good Ole Days

Quitting Drinking vs Falling in Love with Sobriety

Benefits of Being Sober

PART 3-Living a Better Life Sober and Healthy

Changing Lives Health and Wellness

Quitting Drinking and Losing Weight

JOHN EPIFANIO

The Sober Mindset and Some Facebook Group Posts

A Recent Visit by Friends Involving Excessive Alcohol Consumption (Insanity Exemplified) and Some Other Observations

My Typical Loop of Drinking

Do You Need to go to AA?

Non Alcoholic Beer, Wine and Spirits

Introduction

There I was, back from my Christmas vacation sitting in my office with a pounding headache and the heaviest weight

I have ever been in my life. My gut hanging over my belt and heart racing after walking up 4 flights of stairs to my office. I said to myself "Surely, like I did last year I can cut back now and lose a few pounds and yes, I should also moderate my drinking". After all, I had just overindulged on our family holiday cruise (and rightfully so!) because I paid for the "Ultimate Drink Package", drinking at least 10 drinks a day and eating pizzas, burgers, ice cream, 2 entrees for dinner, desserts and more. This is not the first time I was in this position - I actually did the exact same thing the prior year.

Over the years, I sank well into my comfort zone of tasty food and daily alcohol. Bars, casinos (I live in the resort town of Atlantic City, NJ), brew pubs, fast food, happy hours, wineries were all my "reward" for working hard. I have (for the most part) always had a pretty good work ethic and have earned an above average salary. So why would I ever want to change this lifestyle? What else is there to do with my time and money anyway? It was only when I was well into my middle age years did I realize that I had a problem and my health was suffering and I was getting fat, out of shape and generally feeling like crap all the time.

I have decided to write a book at age 54 because of some recent positive and major changes that have improved my life 100%. Disclaimer right up front - In no way do I consider myself to be an expert in the field of nutrition or substance abuse recovery. There are many who write these books who are just that - experts- and far more qualified than me to write about these subjects in terms of what is involved from a medical, psychological or physiological standpoint. Rather, I am writing this book as an honest account of my own experiences, in the hope that it can help others like you. You can lose weight and feel better physically and mentally every day. You can quit drinking and NOT miss it, not even one bit. You can get energy back into your life again for increased happiness, better relationships with spouse, family and friends and better professional/job performance (more success in career). And in my experience, quitting drinking was a natural segue to a relatively quick and safe weight loss and my ticket to all around better health. Now fitting into clothes I haven't worn in years and also weaned off of every prescribed medication I was taking as my blood levels are now near perfect.

In the past half year or so, I have lost over 40 pounds and back down to my college weight via a mentored weight loss program. Additionally, I have given up on a multi-decade problem drinking habit (after a couple failed attempts at "moderation") with the help of some great online resources and books. The result is a monumental increase in mental clarity and an energy level that I never dreamed would be possible to achieve again in my life. By using my own story I aim to help you, the reader, to rediscover how you can also reclaim the energy, focus, money and state of mind that you deserve. Topics to be discussed include:

1) How I quit a decade's long problem drinking career gaining a host of unexpected benefits with absolutely NO downside. Benefits include better sleep, more money in the bank, no hangovers, better quality time with family and friends, improved health, rediscovering old hobbies I had abandoned, more alertness, less stress, and better job performance.
2) My two failed attempts to "moderate"

after successfully quitting drinking and finally understanding why moderation simply does not work.
3) How I lost 40 pounds in a short period of time (and kept it off) by eating healthy and avoiding carbohydrates, sugars, alcohol and processed foods
4) Am I an alcoholic? Do I need to go to AA? What are the other resources available to help me become sober? Are you doomed to a woeful existence giving up the thing you love the most? Or is there a BETTER life out there for you to live?
5) The future plan - staying healthy, keeping the weight off and staying sober. I will share how I got here and what I plan to do to keep on this path for the rest of my life and what you can do to do the same!

Per Merriam Webster:

ADDICTION

a compulsive, chronic, physiological or psychological need for a habit-forming substance, behavior, or activity having harmful physical, psychological, or social effects and typically causing well-defined symptoms (such as anxiety, irritability, tremors, or nausea) upon withdrawal or abstinence : the state of being addicted

ALCOHOLISM

1) continued excessive or compulsive use of **alcoholic**

drinks
2) a chronic, a progressive, potentially fatal disorder marked by excessive and usually compulsive drinking of alcohol leading to psychological and physical dependence or addiction

PART 1 - MY HISTORY AND RELATIONSHIP WITH ALCOHOL

My Early Life

I was born into a loving family of young middle class parents in the late 60's. I reflect on my early years and remember mostly happiness and a warm loving family surrounding me and supporting me from my earliest memories. I had a sense of confidence and eagerness that developed at an early age. I excelled academically and in all things arts and music. I was always near the top of my class and had a gift of musical ability from an early age. I loved singing at school, being in plays and took up the saxophone in 5th grade and progressed pretty quickly to a good skill level. My mother used to commiserate with her friends that while all the other parents were complaining about their child not practicing, "Johnny" would never stop practicing. The sound of the saxophone honking throughout the house was constant and there was no peace and quiet in the house for a couple of years for sure. My parents were young - 19 and 21 at the time of my birth - and did a great job of growing up fast to raise me and my brother Mike who was born two years after me. They established their careers - dad as a salesman for a glass company and mom as a public school teacher. Both of their parents were close by as well as a large extended family all living in my hometown. We enjoyed a solid family foundation for sure, with Sunday dinners and holiday gatherings throughout my younger years. We all start out innocent as life has yet to tempt us with so many pleasures that can ruin lives and lead us to addiction and poor health that results from it.

The First Time

Fortunately, drinking while considered a minor has decreased with each successive generation but most Americans have consumed alcohol before reaching legal drinking age and even while still being a minor (under 18).

In an article written in YouGovAmerica on January 25, 2018 author Hoang Nguyen writes that while the minimum legal drinking age in the US is currently 21, three-quarters of Americans (77%) say they drank for the first time before reaching 21 and six in ten (60%) say they had their first drink while still considered a minor (under 18 years of age). According to YouGov Omnibus data, about one in ten Americans (12%) say they had their first alcoholic drink before the age of 13. About one in five (19%) say they drank for the first time between the age of 13 and 15, and nearly three in ten (29%) say they had their first drink between the age of 16 and 18. That accounts for the six in ten Americans who have had alcohol by the time they have reached adulthood. 17% of Americans drink their first sip of alcohol between the ages of 19 and 21. Only 12% say they had their first drink over the age of 21.

Nearly two-thirds of men (65%) had their first drink

while considered a minor, compared to 55% of women. One-fifth of women (20%) say they drank for the first time between 19 and 21 years of age, compared to just 15% of men at that same age range.

A generational divide exists when it comes to first drinks. Americans between the ages of 45 and 54 are most likely to say they drank as a minor, at 69%. Today's youngest adults report the lowest rate of drinking as a minor, with 41% of 18- to 24-year-olds and 58% of 25- to 34-year-olds saying they drank before the age of 18.

My first memory of drinking alcohol was probably when I was around 10 or 11, but one sip and I learned my lesson (at least for a while). I distinctly remember having a friend over and sitting in front of the liquor cabinet. What are these mysterious bottles which were filled with some kind of adult-only beverage that we are not allowed to try until many, many years later? We had to try it! Just a sip. As children, we knew it was forbidden and it made it all that much more tempting just to try it once. Then finally one day, the first sip... Ewww, blahh! We both spit it right out. How can anyone drink this? I will NEVER drink this. I can never, ever learn to like this and it tastes like poison! It's funny that later in life I would come to feel this way again, the same hatred of it when I finally embraced sobriety once and for all in my 50's. But the multi-decade period of time *in between* is entirely another story.

High School

Fast forward a couple years to high school and now I was really grown up. I now had some older friends and that opened up a whole new world of opportunities for me, a young man who just couldn't wait to "grow up" and experience all the pleasures that life had to offer me. When my parents went away on an overnight trip (I was probably in 9th grade), I somehow ended up alone in the house and invited a couple of the older boys over. I can't remember how I schemed for this to happen, but it did. My father collected pinball machines, so we had an "arcade" in the basement. In addition to a dozen pinball machines, we also had a jukebox and a pool table. This was the place to be. This particular night we were intent on "getting buzzed" and one guy brought over a bottle of Scotch. I remember the nasty taste and even remember to this day the glass from the kitchen I drank it from. It tasted so bad. I remember the room starting to spin and me starting to fall all over the place until I ended up in bed at a very early hour. I still remember the two guys complaining about what a lightweight I was. They were nervously attending to me as I was in my bed and soon vomiting. It was scary but somehow I survived without medical care and we all escaped without being found out and avoided any kind of punishment. This would be my first time drunk.

One particular "friend" from that first night was 17 and thus was in possession of the coveted driver's license and a car. This was the ticket to freedom from my "overprotective" parents once and for all. They knew this friend and were not particularly fond of him to put it mildly. With a little creativity, however (because I was pretty clever in my own way), I could arrange outings with this friend and "cruise" through town in his car with him just riding around aimlessly. What's more, he had a fake ID and could buy alcohol with no problem at all. For most of that year, we would go parking in a field near my home. We would sit in this field in his parked Impala listening to loud rock music and polishing one beer after another. I would buy a six pack of Michelob or Elephant beer and try to drink it all over the course of the night. I would stagger in the house just before my 10 p.m. curfew. This was my first experience getting drunk and also vomiting from over-drinking (I usually got nauseous and puked after beer number 4). This was my first foray into drinking to excess on a somewhat routine basis as this became an almost once a week occasion for quite a while. It was at this young age that I started to develop a tolerance for alcohol. Even though this was limited to just 3-5 times per month on weekend nights, the seed was planting for problem drinking that would develop later in life.

College and The Marijuana Years

Marijuana was recently legalized in NJ and it seems now you can't go anywhere without smelling it. During my later years of my problem drinking, I thought it would be great if I could somehow transition some of my drinking into pot smoking. If not all, at least some of my getting high for fun could be achieved with pot rather than booze. Maybe I would be able to lose a little weight or even sleep better. I bought some and tried "vaping" it too so people around me couldn't smell it, but I couldn't get into it at all. I needed to drink. I always ended up throwing it out as it never really gave me the effect I was searching for.

But when I was in my teens, I got hooked on weed right away. Early in my teens and during a sleepover at my friend's house, he had a joint and asked me to try. I obliged and thus started a new passion of mine, getting "high". By the time I was a senior in high school and into my college years (most of them actually) I got high on pot on a very regular basis. I was an academic standout student (Honor's Business MBA Program at Temple University in Philadelphia) and I was able to keep this part of my life pretty much on the "down low". . I drank too, which may have bordered on problem drinking, but nowhere near the problem it became in later years. At that time, it was mostly about getting high. I thought it was cool and it kind of helped my creativity as well as I was really starting to get into my music as a keyboard player playing in bands. I also listened to a lot of music, and the marijuana usage just sort of went hand-in-hand with that.

Now that I am older and wiser, I shake my head about the time I wasted with this drug. It robbed me of a lot of opportunity and I do not feel it is a "harmless" drug that can be used for recreation. Why would anyone ingest a drug into their system for the purpose of "recreation"? Whatever happened to walking in the park, going to the beach, swimming, biking, family outings…the addict simply doesn't want to hear it. I know many people may feel differently about Mary Jane and that is an individual's choice. And of course there are those that use the drug for real medical reasons-like relief from the pain of glaucoma, which I can completely understand (although before it's legalization I have known a few to get a medical marijuana card under false pretenses). There is much debate over if it is a "real drug" or not and whether it is truly harmful to one's health or not. So I say to each his own on the matter but it cost me a lot in terms of my potential in my formative years. Too many times I chose to get stoned and didn't face the challenge at hand or pursue the next logical growth opportunity. It is also sometimes referred to as a "gateway" drug to harder stuff. The idea being that if you feel this good on a somewhat mild drug, imagine how much better a stronger drug would be. I wish I never met the drug personally. Let alone alcohol!

All Grown Up, Drinking for Fun and "Crossing the Line"

I graduated college in 1989 and was thin as a rail with unbridled energy. I started my own business (a local music store), played music on the side, got married, and got a home. I discovered comfort food and alcohol on the weekends was a lot of fun. In the first couple of years in my new adult life I would gain about 30 pounds and really start enjoying drinking. I had not "crossed the line" quite yet with alcohol - but it was coming.

After a few years firmly rooted in my adulthood, the drinks came easier and easier and I started to really enjoy the "taste" of alcohol. I was looking for events that involved drinking and staying away from events where I could not drink. I bought more and more alcohol to keep in the house and was always persuading my wife to join me for a drink.

I developed an interest in brewing my own beer and bought all the equipment. Then I decided to make my own wine. Looking back, both were not good at all and were more expensive than just buying the real thing made by the professional drink manufacturers. But it was a newfound experience for me that also perfectly justified my growing addiction. If I could somehow produce it myself and share it with friends and family then I was justified in making this bad tasting poison.

My weekends started centering around alcohol more and more. Mainly out of boredom. This was the Blockbuster Video era and it was a great way to spend a Sunday. A couple of DVD's and a couple bottles of wine (at least). I would soon add drinking to my weeknights and eventually up the amount of intake as my tolerance grew. With drinking, the drug demands more and more to just get you to the same level of intoxication. Over the years my tolerance grew to an amount that even amazed me. I could sit and drink almost indefinitely, knocking back drink after drink.

Sometime in the late 90's the Martini came back into vogue and we and our particular group of friends really got into it. We drank vodka mixed with all kinds of creative mixes, ultimately poured into a classic martini glass after being ritualistically shaken in a martini shaker with ice. The sound of the shaker was fun and exciting as good times were about to ensue. It was great for the "lightweight" drinkers because the drinks would be watered down and sweetened to the point of somehow tasting good to people who generally don't like the taste of alcohol. I LIKED the taste of alcohol, so having a vodka martini "straight up" was for me. Now I could drink PURE Vodka out in the open in a social setting with no one even batting an eye. After a few of these martinis you are really hammered.

As time went on, with this kind of drinking and no one to reel me in I eventually "crossed the line". As the Stop Drinking Expert and well-known author Craig Beck calls it the "event horizon". This is the point where you can never go back to moderate and occasional drinking. Alas, no amount of time can erase this. You have lost the ability to moderately enjoy a glass of wine or a beer. You can change a cucumber to a pickle, but you can't change a pickle back into a cucumber. It is at this point that moderation becomes fruitless as the body and mind crave the dulling effects of alcohol to nullify the stress of prior drinks consumed. Ergo, the endless loop of alcohol consumption - drinking to just make yourself feel better as the poison is still in your system wreaking havoc on your body's chemistry.

Hitting Close to Home - Losing Loved Ones to Drinking

Ralph

In 1994, not long out of college and my first job working for Barnett Bank in Jacksonville, FL (which I hated), I decided to open up a local music store selling instruments and music lessons in my hometown of Vineland, NJ. Upon graduating college I wanted to either be 1) A rock star 2) a lawyer, or 3) a music store owner. I chose door #3, the one with the path of least resistance. To get my start, I purchased an established music store - Fiocchi's Music, of which I was a customer and also a part time music teacher. I basically got a bank loan and purchased the building and the inventory from the owner, Al, who was retiring. I also inherited the manager of the store - Ralph - who I believed to be the greatest asset. Ralph was about 10 years older than me and we were already pretty good friends. He had sold me a lot of keyboards over the years and really knew his music, instruments and (most importantly) how to sell. I gave him a job and he also was my tenant in the upstairs apartment. We hit the ground running with the business and it was right when the whole Nirvana/Pearl Jam thing was happening in rock music, so guitars were really popular. We signed up a lot of students those first few years and sold a lot of guitars and related equipment and accessories. We had the full support of the local community and word spread quickly about our cool products and great staff of music instructors. Business was booming and growing.

But I began to notice a problem with Ralph. Some days he just seemed "off". He would say silly things, or be unusually clumsy. His hands would shake and sometimes his speech was off or he'd be uncharacteristically quiet. Then it started getting worse, a lot worse. He was now coming in many days incoherent and I had to send him home a couple of times. I finally had to fire him. But he had me over a barrel. We were so invested in each other. He had a very good skill set for being effective in my business and had a following of customers. He was also my tenant and his rent helped me carry the building financially. His life was the store and he had no other ambitions but to continue being the manager of the local music store. He and his wife divorced shortly before I noticed this being a problem, but apparently his problem was big enough to end his marriage. I had NO IDEA about addictions at that point. I couldn't understand why he couldn't just stop. So I started to visit him at home in an attempt to "fix him". I would have conversations ranging from positive pep talks to threatening ones warning him of his imminent doom if he didn't change his ways. Several times he would promise to get better and I would rehire him only for him to let me and the rest of the staff down once again. The apartment was a mess. It stunk and he stunk. He was flat broke, no food in the refrigerator. It didn't much matter because he wasn't eating anyway even after I bought him groceries that were eventually thrown out. I was "enabling" him and didn't even realize it.

I decided to call AA with him right there with me. I remember a man answering the phone in a very calm voice - I could tell right away he had many years in the program and many years of sobriety. I was determined to solve this problem and explained the problem I was having with Ralph and the urgency to cure Ralph asap. Where can I drop him off, like tonight! Much to my dismay he explained to me that the alcoholic has to make the decision for himself to get better. HE is the only one that can do it.

So this loop of firing then hiring, everyone trying to save him with that great conversation, then him letting everyone down the very next day, etc. continued for a while until one day I got the call that an ambulance picked Ralph up at the apartment. He drank himself into a coma with multiple major issues. Within days he was "brain dead" and I had been named his Health POA. I directed them to stop the feeding tube and he died shortly after at 43 years of age. Premature death 100% caused by alcohol.

Dad

My dad Jack was a great dad and I miss him terribly. He was a hard working man with a sales job for most of his career at Wheaton Glass, landing top salesman many of those years. This was an old school sales job with a lot of travel and a big expense account. Fancy dinners and a lot of drinking with coworkers and customers were the norm. Dad is still remembered to this day as being funny, irreverent, a rascal, jokester and in my opinion a little crazy (but in a good way). He danced to his own drummer, so to speak. He was proud of his sales career and had done very well providing for his family. His identity, in his mind, was his job. So when the company let him go in a surprise reorganization in the late 90's he was absolutely devastated. The company would be sold off shortly afterward. He was able to get another job in the industry but it was not the same. It didn't resemble the job he had at Wheaton at all and the pay was much less. Eventually he would enter early retirement where he assisted me and my brother with our businesses and did some part time jobs. But he was not over "getting downsized" which was his euphemism for being put out to pasture. He fell into a deep depression, intensified his drinking and started acting out irrationally toward family members and friends. His drinking seemed to intensify the oddities in his character, no doubt revealing deep-seated issues he carried with him for decades. He wore his heart on his sleeve with absolutely no filter. He would pick a person to "unload on" and after getting tired of them, would move on to the next person. He and my mom separated and I feared for my mom's life on many occasions after hearing him rant on and on during one of his frequent tirades. I felt that extreme violence was not out of his grasp with his drinking. He was driving drunk all the time and finally got in an accident where fortunately no one was seriously injured. Of course, he somehow was able to elude a DWI charge when in fact he was clearly at least twice the legal limit. This guy had 9 lives I swear. With the intensified drinking and depression deepening those close to him were forced to finally avoid him and let him do whatever it was that he was going to do. He was unpredictable, unhappy and unsafe to both him and people in his life that had "let him down". He was capable of violence for sure and on April 29, 2010 at the age of 64 got inebriated with alcohol and jumped to his death from the 6th floor balcony of his condominium. I remember the call from the police and my first question was "was anyone else hurt"? No, it was a solo job. I was the first one back to the condo before anyone else saw it. The place was a wreck. Food and clothes laying all around. Lights were on and the toilet was full of vomit. Once again, a premature death - 100% caused by alcohol.

Ralph had taught me what addiction really was, so when the problem surfaced with my father several years later I knew that the addict is the only one that can "fix" himself. Both had tried AA and my father had also been committed to a psychiatric facility and also an inpatient detox. All were unsuccessful for both men, as it is for so many addicts. Knowing both men very well, it is my belief that neither of them really wanted sobriety and a better life. In Ralph's case, I remember he told me that he hated the taste of alcohol. When I asked him his nightly routine toward the end, he said he would come home from work and without even taking his coat off would guzzle vodka till he passed out. I believe that they both drank to escape and were very well aware that there was no way out of their situations alive. Both drank themselves to death in spite of countless loved ones trying to intercede and help. Both suffered with psychiatric issues as the drinking progressed. Ralph was deep into hallucinations, seeing people in his apartment and telling strange stories as if they were true, when he was lucid just minutes before. My father continued to struggle with reality and was incapable of any normal relationship with people at the end. He was so bitter and depressed.

PART 2-THE PROBLEM: QUITTING AND MODERATION ATTEMPTS

The Problems Brought on by Drinking

Early on in our drinking careers, the problems that stem from drinking can be relatively benign. For many people, the day after a good night of drinking is not a problem. With a good breakfast and plenty of fluids they are back to their old self in no time. It may be some time before the next drinking session so the pain is easily forgotten. But for the problem drinker chasing the buzz just to get back to feeling somewhat normal due to recent drinking activities, the problems brought on by drinking are a bit more serious.

Short term problems - Anxiety, Sexual difficulties such as impotence (ED), Impaired judgement leading to accidents and injuries, Slowed breathing and heartbeat, Loss of consciousness, Suffocation through choking on your own vomit (Aspiration), Potential poisoning, Blackouts, DWI risk, Making a general ass of yourself,

Overspending, Poor diet choices while drinking, Hangovers causing unproductive and painful "Day Afters", Difficulty remembering things said and done while drinking.

Long term problems - Damage to an unborn child, Liver Disease, Osteoporosis (thinning of the bones), Pancreatitis, Stomach ulcers, Infertility, Heart Disease, Raised Blood Pressure, Stroke, Dimensia, Brain Damage, Continuing reliance on the drug (ethanol), general lowering of your standards, social plans centering around drinking (affecting choice of friends), many other potential health problems like increase in blood sugar A1C, weight gain, poor sleep, loss of brain cells and deteriorating mental capacity.

Short term health risks of alcohol include:
- Anxiety
- Sexual difficulties such as impotence
- Impaired judgement leading to accidents and injuries
- Slowed breathing and heartbeat
- Loss of consciousness
- Suffocation through choking on your own vomit (aspiration)
- Potentially fatal poisoning

The good news is that the short term effects of drinking are reversible. When you reduce your drinking, the symptoms improve.

Long term health risks which alcohol can contribute to:
- Damage to an unborn child
- Liver disease
- Osteoporosis (thinning of the bones)
- Pancreatitis
- Stomach ulcers
- Infertility
- Heart disease
- Raised blood pressure
- Stroke
- Dementia
- Brain damage

Cancer

Alcohol has been classified as a Group 1 carcinogen (carcinogenic to humans) for decades by the International Agency for Research on Cancer. It's right up there with tobacco and asbestos. Alcohol is also a top cause of preventable cancer after smoking and obesity.

From cancer.org (American Cancer Society website):

Alcohol use is one of the most important preventable risk factors for cancer, along with tobacco use and excess body weight. Alcohol use accounts for about 6% of all cancers and 4% of all cancer deaths in the United States. Yet many people don't know about the link between alcohol use and cancer.

Cancers linked to alcohol use

Alcohol use has been linked with cancers of the:

- Mouth
- Throat (pharynx)
- Voice box (larynx)
- Esophagus
- Liver
- Colon and rectum
- Breast

Alcohol probably also increases the risk of cancer of the stomach, and might affect the risk of some other cancers as well.

For each of these cancers, the more alcohol you drink, the higher your cancer risk. But for some types of cancer, most notably breast cancer, consuming even small amounts of alcohol can increase risk.

Cancers of the mouth, throat, voice box, and esophagus: Alcohol use clearly raises the risk of these cancers. Drinking and smoking together raises the risk of these cancers many times more than drinking or smoking alone. This might be because alcohol can help harmful chemicals in tobacco get inside the cells that line the mouth, throat, and esophagus. Alcohol may also limit how these cells can repair damage to their DNA caused by the chemicals in tobacco.

Liver cancer: Long-term alcohol use has been linked to an increased risk of liver cancer. Regular, heavy alcohol use can damage the liver, leading to inflammation and scarring, which might be why it raises the risk of liver cancer.

Colon and rectal cancer: Alcohol use has been linked with a higher risk of cancers of the colon and rectum. The evidence for this is generally stronger in men than in women, but studies have found the link in both sexes.

Breast cancer: Drinking even small amounts of alcohol is linked with an increased risk of breast cancer in women. Alcohol can raise estrogen levels in the body, which may explain some of the increased risk. Avoiding or cutting back on alcohol may be an important way for many women to lower their risk of breast cancer.

The article goes on to say that "ethanol" is the alcohol found in alcoholic drinks and it does not matter whether the drink is beer, wine or spirits. The cancer risk is the same. Overall, the amount of alcohol someone drinks over time, not the type of alcoholic beverage, seems to be the most important factor in raising cancer risk. Most evidence suggests that it is the ethanol that increases the risk, not other things in the drink.

Sleep

Sleep is a big problem when drinking alcohol. Many people believe (erroneously) that drinking actually helps them sleep. In actuality, nothing could be further from the truth. Alcohol is the ultimate sleep disruptor. It may help with initially falling asleep, but only because of the depressant effects of alcohol basically knocking you out. But as we drink, the brain counteracts the depressant by producing a stimulant to "keep you in the game". The alcohol that is now in your system will wreak havoc with your normal sleep patterns and cause you to have terrible sleep. Waking up in the middle of the night once the soporific, sleep inducing initial effects have worn off is commonplace as your body fights to find a chemical equilibrium by releasing stimulants into your system to counteract the depressants. REM sleep (the lighter and less restful sleep associated with dreaming) is drastically reduced after drinking and leads to a very poor quality sleep lacking in the restorative properties found in a good night's sleep. The drinker finds himself wide awake at 4 a.m. wishing for sleep as the 6 a.m. alarm is not too far off. The mind starts to wander and all one can see is all the problems that "could" lie ahead, adding more stress to the moment. Now you really can't sleep at all. When it finally rings, a hungover and exhausted you is forced to face the day in terrible condition.

Alprazolam to Help with Sleep

When I was going through a particularly rough patch in the late 2000's with some investment properties losing value suddenly due to the real estate market crashing, I was prescribed Alprazolam (a version of Xanax) for anxiety. It was tough seeing so much of my hard earned equity evaporate so quickly and I was freaking out with anxiety for the first time in my life. Although the anxiety would eventually pass, I kept taking the drug as it helped me to sleep after drinking.

Alprazolam, more commonly known by the brand name Xanax, is an anti-anxiety and panic disorder medication. Alprazolam is part of a class of drug called **benzodiazepines**, which have the potential to be addictive. "Benzos" I believe is the street term. In a similar fashion, alcohol is a **central nervous system depressant**, and drinking in combination with alprazolam can result in fatal respiratory depression—or dangerously slowed breathing. Alcohol and alprazolam both potentiate the activity of the inhibitory neurotransmitter gamma-aminobutyric acid (GABA) in the brain. This neurotransmitter is responsible for muting widespread excitation in the brain and, when its actions are ramped up, can result in sedation. When these depressants are mixed together, over-sedation may occur—a serious problem that can progress to **coma or even death**. Eventually, I would see this danger for what it was and quit this potentially deadly combination. But when you are a problem drinker, you will take many unnecessary risks with your health. And do ANYTHING for a good night's sleep, because quitting drinking is simply not an option.

I Got This Now, I Can Have Just One

There is so much truth to the statement "one drink is too many and 1000 is never enough" (or variations thereof). Once you "cross the line", and your brain has learned that alcohol is the answer to the unsettled feeling that is happening in your body (brought on by the prior drink), it is almost impossible to forget it is there and will provide you with a quick remedy for the way you are feeling. As erroneous as this thinking is, it is hard to unlearn this. The drink will cause the stress anew and its relief is very fleeting. Then that drink creates new stress where another drink is needed to make you feel better. And so it goes, the endless loop of problem drinking. This exact process is described very well in William Porter's "Alcohol Explained" Book 1. Book 2 is also an excellent book. I highly recommend both books.

People can go a long time (sometimes many years) in sobriety and start to dream about the idea of moderation. "I think I can now have just one drink - I've got this now". For me, I love eating out and having a nice Italian meal with a nice big glass of red wine. Or cooking my own

Italian meal while drinking red wine. It's just something that I have done for a long time and it has always been very therapeutic. So twice now, I have flirted with the idea of moderating my drinking after relatively long periods of sobriety. Both times ended with me ending right back to drinking at the level of when I last stopped drinking (maybe even more drinking). Here is how my two attempts to moderate went (3 TIMES QUITTING):

My Failed Moderation Attempts

Brief overview:

End 2017 Quit after a multi-decade problem drinking career, sober ALL of 2018, beginning 2019 resumed drinking ALL 2019, beginning 2020 through June 2020 quit, resumed July 2020 and drank till Jan 2022, then QUIT and so far so good!

Attempt to Quit (then Moderate) #1:

At the end of 2017 I went on a cruise and purchased the drink package, basically allowing me to drink unlimited amounts of alcohol at any time of the day, all day, every day. So I did just that, drank non stop - an insane amount of alcohol by most people's standards. Upon checking out of the room on the morning of departure, I was amazed to see that I had consumed 100 alcoholic drinks on my 7 day cruise. My typical day started at about 6:30 with a couple of Bloody Marys. Then to the pool for sugar laden rum-filled Bahama Mamas. Then lunch, afternoon snack with a couple Martinis maybe, dinner with 2-3 glasses of wine, then shows with a couple of drinks, and maybe more nightcaps after. The alcohol all the while increasing my appetite to eat anything and everything. I probably gained 10 pounds on that cruise and felt like absolute crap.

Here's how it works:

Alcohol increases weight because it is a fuel that the body must burn so any food in your system is usually turned to fat as there is nothing else the body can use it for. Then you have the extra empty calories of alcohol and any sugar with the mixers. Empty calories are called "empty" because they offer absolutely NO nutritional value whatsoever. And the sugar in most mixers is just another type of poison. Then you have the bad eating decisions you make when you are drunk. Your body craves certain vitamins and minerals it is now lacking and the brain compensates by eating junk food (sometimes late at night). Your system is confused and is consuming everything in sight at this point in order to satisfy the craving brought on by whatever it is deficient in. Again, the drunken mind is acting irrationally, so the drinker just overeats and consumes all the wrong food.

But I digress, back to the story...

So coming home I decided maybe this isn't normal and it was time to do something about it. I stumbled upon a YouTube channel called "The Stop Drinking Expert" by

Craig Beck and have been a fan ever since. I have read his book "Alcohol Lied to Me" and have watched all his YouTube videos. For those trying to quit and rid their lives of this poison, I highly recommend him. His course, book "Alcohol Lied to Me" and his YouTube channel changed my life. With the info I learned from his book and videos I now had the tools to finally stop drinking after almost daily drinking for almost 30 years. I quit for all of 2018, not a drop. Every holiday, birthday party, wedding, funeral, golf outing, you name it, I was sober as could be. But I still had a "screw loose" and even though my life had dramatically improved in so many ways, I was not fully satisfied with my now sober existence. I still missed the way it made the party, the reward it promised at the end of a stressful day, the way it eased conversations in social settings. The way the glass of Chianti went hand in glove with spaghetti and meatballs I made on a Sunday afternoon. Actually it was the two glasses I had preparing the food, the one I had with dinner, and the one I took back to the couch after dinner - boom, a whole bottle.

So in the beginning of 2019, the dreaded 5 words were said in my head "Just One Drink Won't Hurt". You see, I had clearly "beaten" this addiction in my mind. Maybe it wasn't even an addiction after all, I had quit so easily anyway, right? And maybe I was being a little dramatic with my health concerns. I was in fairly decent shape for my age after all. I would later come to learn this is what William Porter, author of "Alcohol Explained" (another highly recommended book) calls The Fading Affect Bias, or FAB for short. It refers to the cognitive phenomenon supported by research showing that memories associated with negative emotions tend to fade faster than memories associated with positive emotions. This means we tend to forget the bad times at a faster rate than the good times. Then guess what, my problem got worse than ever. After a few weeks of "moderating" I was right back to where I left off. Fueling my body daily with more booze to relax myself and to relieve the symptoms of my last drink. Caught in the endless cycle. Day in and day out. Waking up with a hangover, bloated, putting on weight, eating when I wasn't hungry because of the drinking and not having any energy to do anything. Just surviving. I live in Atlantic City, NJ and the casinos are 5 minutes away from me. You can play slots or Black Jack and get free drinks here. In my final few months of this period I was going to the Hard Rock Casino pretty routinely for 3 free martinis to start the day around noon. Some days I took off and started "vacation vodka drinking" in the morning.

After a full year of returning to drinking in 2019, my health started to take a turn for the worse toward the end of the year. I made the dreaded misstep that so many quitters make - I thought I could moderate and thought I could drink normally. Again drinking was out of hand, daily drinking was the norm. So much for my moderation plan. I developed a dull pain in my left front rib cage and thought it was diverticulitis or some kind of gastrointestinal issue but my doctor said it was probably nothing after we had an x-ray and ultrasound done. He could not find any issue. I had a pain in my left side near my rib cage. The x rays did find a fatty liver, to which the doctor recommended an improved diet (which I would address later with my commitment to my weight loss/health plan). I can still feel a dull pain there but not the shooting pain I experienced when I was drinking. I am convinced this is long term damage to my digestive tract due to years of drinking. I am hopeful that it will improve over time. I was constantly hung over in the year 2019 with my weight ballooning up to over 240 as a result of a very poor diet. After an end of the year vacation in which I overindulged in food and drink, I committed to giving up the drink again.

My last day of insanity was 1/17/20. That night I started listening to Craig Beck's videos again. The first 4-5 days of detox was very tough for me. I was experiencing big time insomnia and I was out of my Alprazolam. I had been using Alprazolam (1 MG at bedtime) for approximately 10 years to help me sleep through the night, and this is a habit I have since quit. Drinking alcohol simply knocks out the drinker for several hours as the brain secretes depressants but then wakes up the drinker around 4 am as the brain attempts to reach an equilibrium and secretes stimulants to counter the depressive alcohol effects. The result is a crappy night sleep with very little REM sleep (the kind of sleep where much of the dreaming is done and is needed for a deep, restorative sleep). The Alprazolam was my "trick" to stay asleep as I previously mentioned, but a very risky "solution" that I consider myself lucky to have escaped alive. The warnings are very clear to not mix the drug with alcohol.

I also experienced, on one of these initial nights, a shooting pain in the back of my left leg that kept me up all night (although I probably wouldn't have slept anyway with all the stimulants in my body and also the sheer terror of whether or not I was dying at that moment being very present).

My blood pressure was raging. The poison was still in me after 4-5 days of not drinking. I got bloodwork done.

(Thank God it came back with no issues.). I was very disoriented for several days too and it was hard to work and concentrate. I was sleep deprived and feared cancer or liver issues. I finally felt better around day 7. This sucked. I said to myself "Don't drink anymore, you will fall back into it and everything starts to suck again." So now at the beginning of 2020, I was finally back on track and instantly got more productive and life started to improve in every way once again.

Attempt to Quit (then Moderate) #2:

2020 started off sober again and even with the boredom of the ensuing COVID lockdown I did not give in to the temptation of the drink. However, the abstinence would only last 6 months this second time around and I eventually decided to moderate once again in July 2020, convinced I could really do it this time around. But wrong again, within a very short time I was back to the daily drinking, daily hangovers, stress and feeling like crap.

Finally Quit Attempt #3

Back to drinking from July 2020 through all of 2021. Same old shit once again, not able to moderate. Blackouts from drinking too much, falling out of bed. Walking into the closet on the way back from the bathroom and waking up in said closet. Snoring and sweating profusely during sleep. Tossing, turning and unable to sleep. Relying on prescription drugs for sleep. 10 hours in bed "sleeping" and waking up groggy and still tired. Alcohol is the ultimate robber. Finally on Jan 19, 2022I decided that the 3rd and final time was enough. Drinking in moderation cannot be an option for a drinker like me who "crossed that line" many years ago. It is time to embrace a new beginning, a lifestyle free of the bonds of being addicted to a poison that steals your health, time, money and energy and gives nothing in return.

The Good Ole Days

The memories of throwing back a few cold ones with the buddies are just that - memories. I have found that some things (like alcohol) are better left as memories even when they do not present a danger to us. For example, I loved to SCUBA dive in the early 2000's. I spent a lot of time getting certified to dive and even achieved my PADI master scuba certification. I made so many friends and memories diving and visited many interesting places. However, as the years went on, I dove less and less but would still try to go every year or two to keep my skills up. On those trips, I realized the fun was gone and probably will not return. I will probably never get the same joy out of that activity again. Perhaps it was the time and circumstances that surrounded me at the time I learned that made it so special. I remember it fondly when I reflect on it. I remember certain trips taken, the friends I made, the sites I dove at, dinners and drinks after a dive, etc. I look back with the rosiest colored glasses and now realize I forget all the negatives I used to hate. It was expensive, I got nauseous and threw up a lot while on the dive boat, I was cold on a lot of dives. Many dives were boring and I was seeing the same things over and over again. For some reason we tend to remember the good memories, not the inconveniences or negative aspects, as time goes on. This is what author

William Porter calls "Fading Affect Bias". Like SCUBA diving, realizing this key point - THOSE DAYS ARE OVER - was critical in my final decision to quit drinking and it will serve you well to understand this in your own attempt to change your life for the better and eliminate the poison from your life once and for all.

That time is gone and will never return again no matter how great the memories are and how much I wish for those times again. However, there are still great things to experience and accomplish in this life that are new and exciting for me. Like writing this book for example or going out for rides on my new boat. I now have a son that I didn't have when I dove, so I now get to do new and exciting things with him and see these things through his eyes. No matter how much I try to either dive or drink, I will never come close to reaching the stuff that lives in my memory.

Quitting Drinking vs Falling in Love with Sobriety

As I continue to lead a fulfilling and productive life free from the bonds of alcohol, nothing irritates me more than someone hearing my story and pitying the fact that I can't drink or don't want to drink anymore. Alcohol is indeed the only drug we have to justify NOT taking. Not only is it assumed that we are somehow "damaged" or "broken" if we don't imbibe, but are now to be felt sorry for. How pathetic is this? How can any logical, normal person NOT get addicted to a highly addictive substance that is constantly being pushed on all of us and has billions of marketing dollars spent by the alcohol industry promoting it as normal, fashionable, sexy, macho, etc.?

I have been a musician all my life and love all kinds of music. I enjoy listening to country music as well. It is laughable, however, the titles of songs and lyrical references to alcohol in so many country songs in particular. Some of my favorites:

1) Drunk on a Plane - Dierks Bentley
2) Drinking Beer Talking God Amen - Chase Rice/Florida Georgia Line
3) Alcohol You Later - Mitchell Tenpenny
4) Tequila Makes Her Clothes Come Off - Joe Nichols
5) Drink on it - Blake Shelton
6) AA - Walker Hayes

I think you get the idea. Getting drunk is so ingrained in our culture at every turn.

So how exactly do we react to the question of "why are you not drinking"? I have found my best response to shut them down is "I don't like the way it makes me feel". I struggle to keep it short, it is in my nature to answer people as completely as possible (to a fault). A simple response is probably the best rather than trying to educate and convert people to being non- drinkers. You also must be mindful that the person asking the question may be seeking validation for their own drinking. I believe I used to be this way. I would want everyone to drink with me. Personally, my social circles are much smaller these days and most people I am socializing with now are familiar with my journey, so I don't need to do much explaining thank goodness.

Quitting drinking is a very admirable thing to do, especially in light of the fact that so many people have drunk for so long. It is a highly addictive substance and only gets worse over time as one's tolerance increases. So no matter what "method" one chooses to quit drinking, it is always an accomplishment that takes a serious commitment and the willingness to change the status quo.

The sober lifestyle has absolutely no downside. In the process of quitting I have had the opportunity to examine all the reasons why I made that decision. I am now proud to admit that I am just "Alcohol Free" now.

Benefits of Being Sober

When I first attempted to quit alcohol in 2018 I made a list of reasons why I wanted to quit and the benefits I believed that would follow when I put the bottle down. Here is the list I wrote:

Spend More Time with Family

Rekindled and new friendships.

Hobbies-Improve or do more: Golf, Scuba, Reading, Piano, Guitar

Travel more, especially day trips

Improved sexual performance

Attend More concerts and Sporting Events

More Energy and no hangovers

Wake up in the morning feeling great with a positive attitude

More $$$$$$$$ (due to not spending on alcohol and also increased productivity at work)

Naturally eat better and have an appetite

Lose weight

Improved Poop Quality

Better sleep

Improved Blood work (Stop the unnecessary meds)

No DWI/DUI risk and available to drive at any time (should an emergency pop up)

Eliminate Bad Breath and/or alcohol breath

No more constant heat flashes and racing heart

No more snoring

Overall more Happiness and Less Stress

I am proud to say almost all these things have come true. Committing to a sober existence has its health benefits for sure and life is WAY better in every way without the poison in your life. Here is a recap of where I am with my list of reasons for quitting and my hopes for what would happen in sobriety:

Spend More Time with Family. When you quit drinking you find yourself with a lot more time, as you are not just sitting around most of the time drinking yourself into a stupor. There is now a huge void in your life as far as time that must be filled! And idle time is the devil's time as they say. So it is important to find constructive ways to fill that void left from your "drinking time". In fact, one of the biggest reasons for relapse is that people do not fill up this newfound time with other non-drinking activities. For many, this is both exciting and daunting at the same time. In my case, I have committed to walking/hiking and writing this book. I also enjoy boating and fishing. Find an activity and do it! Stay busy, alcohol is always tempting you with an easy way to spend all your time and you don't want to go back to that.

Rekindled and new friendships. Many of the people on the Facebook sobriety groups I follow, especially younger people it seems, comment on how quitting drinking affects friendships. If your idea of socializing was going clubbing or going to bars or pubs, then there is a good chance you spent most of your time with like minded drinkers. Without drinking it becomes difficult to stay in the same environments carrying on with these people in the same way. Drinkers tend to look to other drinkers to somehow justify their own drinking. When you cease to be that justification for someone they will simply (and maybe unwittingly) move on to someone else who will. You are now an unpleasant reminder to them of the thing they are doing that they know deep down inside is wrong for so many reasons.

For me, I have not had to endure much of this as I am older, a family man, and have a relatively small social circle. The friends I do have I keep because we have a relationship on a much deeper level. My best friend, Steve, still gets together with me to socialize a couple times per month. We have been close for over 25 years now and used to drink every time we got together for many, many years. The drinking stories we have can fill up another book easily. But now, the fact that we are getting older and the fact that I have changed my lifestyle to that of a teetotaler now means we simply do activities together that don't involve drinking. I also have a group of casual friends at my local cigar lounge that I visit a couple times a week, but those conversations are usually limited to the news of the day, sports or music. I shake my head when I think of all the pointless encounters I have had in bars making new "friends"-talking for hours and forming a special bond, where in fact the only thing we had in common was getting a good buzz on. I remember many years ago when I was in between my marriages, I was dating a woman that loved to go to a certain area restaurant that turned into a cocktail lounge with dancing every Wednesday night. Oh how we loved those Wednesday nights. This was at the pinnacle of my martini obsession and they made very good (and expensive) martinis. It would be no problem for us to drink 3-4 of these and they each had about 2-3 shots in them. We would stroll around the bar for hours, martini in hand, greeting all of our "friends" who were doing the same. She was about ½ my weight and would often get very drunk and become a different person by the end of the night. And if I'm being completely honest, maybe I was too. I'll leave it at that, I'm glad we were both able to move on to better relationships.

My sober conversations with my real friends and family are now more genuine and gratifying.
I don't miss getting drunk with my family at family gatherings at all. At some point in my life, family gatherings were great. I was a child and could not wait to see everyone - cousins, aunts, uncles, grandparents. I wanted to see them with the best of intentions. It was great to play sports in the back yard with my cousins, run around, perform my saxophone solos for my great aunts, tell everyone about my school, etc. At some point, I'm thinking probably during the high school graduation era, it became ok to drink at family gatherings. Then eventually it became intolerable not to. Even funerals. Wedding receptions with open bars and hors d'oeuvres

were the best. The problem with excessive drinking at family functions really hit home for me (and was probably the beginning of me questioning my relationship with alcohol) last Thanksgiving when my brother commented about some words said at the dinner table that were no doubt alcohol induced. The person making the comments no doubt said inappropriate things and the person who the comments were made to no doubt overreacted (also alcohol induced) leading to an awkward situation that diminished what should have been and should always be a great, wholesome family time centered around enjoying a great meal together as a family.

Hobbies-Improve or do more: Golf, Scuba, Reading, Piano, Guitar. To be completely honest I suffer from bouts of serious laziness now and things like improving on the musical instruments have heretofore eluded me. Many of the things on the list that involve recreation I realize are just not to be embraced by me now in my new sober existence. I will not rule out diving or golf, but these activities tend to take up a lot of time and are a bit on the pricey side. Perhaps I gave them up due to my drinking habits but now I have just decided to do other things. My family has recently developed a love for hiking and we spend a lot of our free time doing that together.

Travel more, especially day trips. As a family, we have really committed to traveling. We have been doing at least one cruise per year, a trip to Florida once a year, and try to get away on one or two overnight trips every quarter. My travel now has the added benefit of being alcohol free. No longer do I need to schedule my family's vacation around my drinking habit. I am preparing for an upcoming cruise and will NOT be purchasing the drink package, nor will I drink on the cruise. I have probably been on 15 cruises in my life. I WILL be looking forward to filling up my time with excursions this time whereas I have been content to just stay on board and drink on past cruises. It will be great to create these lasting memories with the family this time. The last two cruises I completed I came home feeling like absolute crap and serious weight gained, I am looking forward to changing that this time.

Improved sexual performance. Absolutely an improvement post drinking. Excessive alcohol consumption makes it hard to get an erection and also sustain an erection. This is called ED or Erectile Dysfunction. Basically there are two reasons why this happens -1) The alcohol interferes with the messengers in the brain that tell the penis to fill with blood and 2) Alcohol can interfere and lower the production of testosterone, which is the hormone that controls male sexual functions. And who really wants to be intimate with a sloppy drunk. Slurring their words, saying stupid things, clumsy, tired and not in the moment. Alcohol is a very self centered drug, it will steal everything including the intimacy so important for a successful and mutually fulfilling romantic relationship.

Attend more concerts and sporting events: As a musician myself, attending concerts is something I used to do often. However, now the idea of driving over an hour each way, parking, sitting with a big, unpredictable crowd of screaming idiots, overpaying for tickets, etc. has no appeal to me anymore. I will take the family to a nice classical music concert or theater, but those are few and far between. Also, I hate how they rip off people with prices anymore. From the concert tickets, to parking to the price of concessions. We live in Philadelphia Eagles football country here in South Jersey. Yesterday a friend asked me if I wanted first crack at some upcoming game tickets. I texted him back and politely declined the 4 tickets at $175 each (also parking is $40), gas and tolls $25, beers are now $11 and hot dogs are $8. All this to sit in the cold on a plastic seat and watch a very slow moving game. I'd much rather sit at home and watch the game on my big screen where it is nice and warm, no driving required, the cost is free, and I get to hear the announcers "play by play" and can use my own bathroom or get snacks from my kitchen during the commercials.

More energy with no hangovers. I wake up now with unbridled energy and a clear head. I used to wake up so depressed and with a negative outlook on life. I stressed about the upcoming day thinking of all the things that could go wrong. Now I loosely plan the structure of my day and let it unfold like a flower.

Wake up in the morning feeling great with a positive attitude It is hard to put a price on the feeling of waking up every morning not hungover and not having alcohol in your system.

More $$$$$$$$ (due to not spending on alcohol and also increased productivity at work). Here is my math. Daily habit of 4-5 drinks (bottle of wine, several beers, or several mixed drinks) approx $15/day. $15 x 365 days = $5,475. Plus one dinner a week out with a drink bill of approx $25. 52 x $25=$1300. Extra few bottles of wine or bottles of spirits on the weekend $30 x 52 = $1300. So conservatively, I am saving at least $8k per year. When I factor in the sober influence I am having on my other housemates (my wife and father-in-law), our family is easily saving a 5 figure number every year. I no longer bring alcohol to family parties as a "gift for the host" either. More so for the principle of it than the cost.

Naturally eat better and have an appetite. So many times I remember trying to skip meals in an attempt to "save calories for drinking". Getting drunk leads to poor food choices and eating late at night as well. By not consuming alcohol and eating whole foods (not processed food) and cutting back on carbs and sugar, you will feel full and actually feel the need to eat less. Since quitting drinking, I don't get that insatiable, ravenous appetite that I used to get.

Lose weight. Upon achieving a sober lifestyle, I lost much more weight than I thought, but I coupled it with a weight loss plan (More discussion of this in Part 3, **Changing Lives Health and Wellness**)

Improved Poop Quality. Alcohol has many different effects on the body, both short- and long-term. It can affect how the body breaks down nutrients, irritate the gut, and speed up the digestive system. Alcohol may make the digestive system work more quickly than usual. As the contents of the stomach will pass through the small and large intestines faster, the body may be unable to absorb the normal amount of water back into the body. This lack of reabsorption can result in a loose, watery stool. After I quit drinking, my stool was back to normal in a short period of time and bowel movements became much more regular and predictable.

Better sleep. Hands down one of the best benefits of quitting drinking. No more passing out drunk only to wake up a few hours later wide awake unable to get back to sleep. As I had hoped, my sleep has returned to normal, usually sleeping mostly straight through the night for 7 to 8 hours.

Improved Blood work (Stop the unnecessary meds). Last week I went to the doctor and I am now off ALL medications. No more high blood pressure, anxiety, or cholesterol medicine. My A1C (the simple blood test that measures your average blood sugar levels over the past 3 months) was in the beginning stage of diabetic at 6.7 six months ago and today it is normal at 5.5. My blood pressure was a perfect 123/80 (historically while I was a drinker I always fought high blood pressure and was even on meds for it for awhile).

No DWI/DUI risk and available to drive at any time (should an emergency pop up) How many times does the drinker get behind the wheel of the automobile knowing that they are probably over the limit and weigh the risk of driving? Staying the night at a friend's house can be embarrassing and is also "admitting" that you overdrank. It is also, oftentimes, an imposition on your host. If you are far away from home, getting a hotel can be a big expense, and you still have to find a way to the hotel. Ubering or getting a taxi is also an expense and you still have to deal with getting your car in the morning. The other factor of being drunk is that if an emergency pops up, you are not able to jump in a car and tend to a family emergency. You must make other plans or risk drunk driving. For me, I still catch myself some nights looking in the rear view mirror for patrol cars eyeing me for swerving - just out of habit. I no longer need to have my wife drive us home after a night out every time "out of an abundance of caution". I am available to drive at a moment's notice 24 hours a day. I am always 100% available to face any situation - driving, consoling, advising, teaching, consulting, loving, parenting, husbanding, counseling, etc. I am sober.

Eliminate Bad Breath and/or alcohol breath. When we drink too much alcohol, our bodies treat the substance as a toxin and convert it to less harmful chemicals to protect us from its damaging effects. About 90% of the alcohol we consume gets converted to acetic acid, and that's what causes bad breath following an alcohol binge. It is also nice to not have to hide alcohol on your breath, which is something I was mindful of for many years.

No more constant heat flashes and a racing heart. Drinking alcohol increases your heart rate. The more you drink, the faster your heart beats. And as we drink, the blood vessels in the skin tend to widen as the heart rate speeds up. This process is called vasodilation. **Dilated blood vessels cause the skin to feel warm and flushed, which can trigger the release of sweat**. This sweating could occur at any time of day. At the height of my drinking career, I would sweat profusely at night, waking up in a pool of sweat with the sheets soaking wet. I would routinely have heart palpitations during the day as well and my blood pressure was sky high. These problems magically went away when I committed to living my life alcohol free.

No more snoring. The muscles in the back of the throat close faster in an intoxicated person than a sober person and explains why someone might snore, or snore louder, when they drink. The more you drink, the more relaxed the tissues and muscles become, and the louder you will snore. According to my doting wife, I no longer snore to any great extent while sleeping. I am sure that if I do it is not as frequent or as loud. Yet another small plus that comes from not drinking.

Overall more Happiness and Less Stress. Being employed in the real estate industry, there are definite ups and downs inherent with my business. As Frank Sinatra sang in "That's Life":

You're riding high in April, shot down in May
But I know I'm gonna change that tune
When I'm back on top, back on top in June

When business is good, life is all unicorns and rainbows, but when it is slow life can become quite stressful. It is easy to chalk up a slow business time to the idea that maybe somehow you are not that great and are in the wrong line of work. Stress compounds this negative outlook and clouds the reality that business and life in general is really cyclical in nature. When I look back on my life I can see this very clearly. Learning to diversify your interests and hobbies no matter what is going on with your professional career has been a key to my happiness recently. When I was at the height of my problem drinking I was routinely waking up at 4 a.m. with my thoughts racing. I could not get to sleep thinking about each deal I had in the works and all the things that could possibly go wrong with them. Now I sleep through the night and wake up refreshed and energized and set out on my day excited and ready to take on the world.

PART 3-LIVING A BETTER LIFE SOBER AND HEALTHY

Changing Lives Health and Wellness

In early 2022 and on the heels of my newfound sobriety I decided to make a deeper commitment to my health. Some local friends of mine who own a local insurance brokerage opened up a business focused on weight loss and improving general health. They recruited an experienced health and wellness coach named Mitch who lost 120 pounds 13 years ago and has kept it off and now helps others do the same. One partner Bobby is the "poster child" for the business and lost 135 pounds in 7 months. The other partner lost 65 pounds in a relatively short period as well. I signed up for the program and lost 33 pounds in 45 days. Total of over 40 pounds in roughly a few months. This was all done safely and without hunger or any kind of excessive exercise. Alcohol is forbidden during the weight loss phase so that only strengthened my resolve not to drink early in my sobriety. Unfortunately, I have had a few friends inquire about this program and when they found out they couldn't drink during the weight loss phase they told me flat out they just couldn't do that.

Being sober AND seeing the weight falling off so quickly at 54 years old was an incredible feeling. Certainly something I thought I would never see. Now that I am many months past the initial weight loss I am happy to say the weight has stayed off. Perhaps it is my newly adopted way of eating but maybe the health benefits of not drinking also. More than likely a combination of both. For me personally, not drinking has added A LOT of leeway for me to eat and not gain weight. I did learn a lot through the weight loss phase and I truly do view food differently and make healthier choices, but I no longer have to be burdened by eating desserts or having that second helping as I know that without alcohol I can do so. And the scale proves it. So what exactly are the weight loss benefits of quitting drinking you ask?

Quitting Drinking and Losing Weight

Alcohol is a fuel that your body will go to first when it needs energy. It is readily available and easy to access. So when you're drinking, all of your caloric intake takes 2nd place to the alcohol in your system. If not burned, the calories you normally consume will turn to fat.

Additionally, alcohol causes us to feel hungrier than we actually are because we crave high calorie foods when we drink, very often not feeling satisfied even after eating a lot. And many times, junk food or greasy food late at night. Maybe a run to McDonalds or a late night pizza delivery.

If we are lacking in certain nutrients, the body will crave them and since alcohol prohibits the absorption of these nutrients we do not feel satisfied, even when we are mostly full.

And due to the lack of quality sleep brought on by drinking and also the stimulant chemicals released in the body to counteract the depressant effects of alcohol, we feel constantly hungry. Since we are tired all the time, the laziness is ever present and a barrier to exercise, thus increasing our calorie in/calorie out daily ratio in favor of weight gain.

It is a fact that after drinking, your ghrelin levels (the hormone that makes you feel hungry) go up and leptin (the hormones that make you feel full) go down.

Once I quit, the weight loss came easy as I wasn't eating unnecessarily. My only exercise was walking and a weekly 15 mile bike ride. I started to drop the weight a couple months before I went on my diet plan. Once I signed up for the weight loss program, my results were positively compounded for the better as I no longer had to fight the anti-weight loss effects that drinking causes. So the low-calorie daily diet WITHOUT alcohol led to me safely losing ¾ of a pound to a full pound a day and feeling great doing it.

The diet was very straightforward, only 3.5 ounces of protein and 3.5 ounces of vegetables twice a day, 2 pieces of fruit, 2 bread sticks or melba toast and plenty of water (or coffee or tea). Unlimited salsa, cucumbers and cabbage. The program administers natural and homeopathic drops that cut down on cravings and give you energy. You are not allowed to have sugar but Stevia or Truvia substitutes are allowed. So on this daily regiment, your body learns to wean itself off the sugar and processed foods that are usually loaded with sugar and fat. You can email me for more information about this program and I will be happy to provide a link. Currently the program is very popular in my community and there are countless success stories piling up of people losing a lot of weight quickly and safely.

These days since I have completed the weight loss and maintenance phases of the program I am basically on the "rest of my life" phase. In this phase, I am mindful of what I eat during the weekdays and do my best to avoid processed foods, carbs and sugar. Definitely no alcohol! Then on the weekends I eat whatever I want. And that I do. Come Monday, I am back to being prudent again.

I did the weight loss program to achieve my desired "forever" weight, and am happy to say that once I reached it it is now relatively easy to maintain with very little sacrifice. Never hungry as I eat all real foods. On occasion I will eat ice cream, cake or chocolate, but mostly go to fruits for the sweet tooth. I do eat a lot of meat and dairy products and I love cheese. I have really cut down on breads, cereal, wraps, etc and definitely no sodas (I never have really drunk soda anyway). I drink a lot of water, coffee and unsweetened tea and occasionally alcohol free beer if I feel like "partying".

I'm not sure if it is just me but I see a lot of people recently who have gone on successful weight loss diets and really have lost weight. Additionally, they have improved their health tremendously. Lower blood sugar, lower A1C, lower blood pressure, lower resting heart rate, lower cholesterol, more energy, better sleep, etc. Add to that cutting out alcohol and you become a totally new person.

To recap from above, alcohol makes you gain weight

because:

1) It is a "fuel" in your body that you will burn first for energy before burning the calories of food you have eaten. Since there is nowhere for those calories to go, the body turns that into fat
2) Alcohol is all "empty calories" with absolutely no nutritional value whatsoever. So the calories you drink are all extra daily calories ingested. Not to mention the sugary mixers used in most drinks
3) After drinking the body will crave vitamin and mineral deficiencies and binge eat to satisfy the cravings, unsure of what it really needs and never really satiating the craving
4) Being drunk means terrible decision making and you eat all the wrong foods at the wrong time. Like late night pizza deliveries, fast food runs and eating a whole bin of ice cream or anything left in the fridge.

My advice to lose weight is to FIRST AND FOREMOST stop drinking. Then pick a diet that will work for you (the above worked miracles for me) and stick to it with the same mindset that you approach your newfound sobriety.

Now, if I could only quit Ice Cream…

The Sober Mindset and Some Facebook Group Posts

I belong to several quit drinking/sober Facebook groups. I find these to be very helpful in maintaining my sobriety. There are wonderful posts from people who have successfully conquered problem drinking and also maintained sobriety for a long time. There are also many posts from people who are constantly tripping up and resetting their sobriety clocks back to Day One as a result of slipping up. What is the difference between these two groups of people? I believe the stumblers are not really grasping the concept that alcohol provides ZERO benefits. They are still chasing the "high" from alcohol that over time becomes ever more elusive. They still feel that by quitting they are somehow missing out on a benefit. Allow me to elaborate with some anonymous, real life examples:

POST: I told a coworker the other day that I'm almost 1 year sober. His response was "wow, you don't LOOK like an alcoholic!" I was a little shocked. Just curious if anyone else has experienced a reaction like that.

ME: This is a great point of discussion as anyone who has decided to take the sober route will inevitably get called out on it by drinkers. Drinkers want EVERYONE to drink with them to justify their errant behavior. As long as everyone else is drinking there is no reason to feel guilty about poisoning yourself with alcohol. People who have decided to lead a sober life may be all over the spectrum. From not really having had a problem and just deciding life is better without it to serious alcoholics who were facing imminent death if they didn't stop. As someone who was somewhere in the middle, I have decided that the best response (when asked why I'm not drinking) is "I'm not in the mood". If still pressed, I may reply with something like "I'm not drinking anymore because I don't like the way it makes me feel so now I'm alcohol free". Or maybe, a lighter approach would be "I've drunk my lifetime limit!". I am not sure if I was ever technically an "alcoholic". I was someone who drank a highly addictive poison for many years and crossed the line with it. And I've got news for you - alcohol is the 2nd most addictive substance on the planet second only to heroin. If anyone, any human, drinks it long enough and consistently enough, they WILL get addicted to it. And another point to be made (and is absolutely crazy) is that in our modern society alcohol is the only drug where we have to explain why we AREN'T drinking rather than why we are. Again, drinkers love to feel like they are part of the mainstream and there is nothing wrong with consuming this poison for the fun of it. But again, I digress...

As I continued to age, my tolerance skyrocketed and my health started to decline and my weight started to increase. So I quit, period. So for anyone to label me as an "alcoholic", feel that I am broken or feel pity for me is out of line and on that I will defend myself till the end. Again, I try not to invite a big discussion about it unless someone is genuinely interested in finding out how I made a change to better myself with my sober path.

POST: Well, I hate to admit it- but I'm falling off the proverbial wagon again.

I was doing quite well for myself for awhile.. I had 4 months in then spiraled when the summer began 😵

Alcohol is proving to be so gosh darn addicting & difficult to quit. It's like I just can't stop itching for it.

& Last night, I REALLY overdid it so I'm suffering badly today. Heart palpitations, pure anxiety, the whole bit..

You'd think i'd learn

ME: Although I can appreciate the honesty, there are many posts that are more of a cry for help than anything else. Sometimes I will add my 2 cents and say something like "There is absolutely nothing beneficial about drinking" and leave it at that. Just let that marinate for a second...enough said.

POST: I think the biggest lie alcohol has you believe is that you have to stop all the activities you did drinking. I call BS! That's why there are other drink options out there.

ME: Excellent point again. You do not have to stop or limit any of the things you did for fun in the past. For example, I own a boat and it has a large cooler built in that drains to the bilge. It is very convenient to climb aboard with drinks, throw them in the cooler with a big bag of ice and you are set for the day. In the past, I used to load it up with all kinds of drinks and encourage everyone to drink on our day out boating. I still have it loaded up with all kinds of drinks (both alcoholic and non alcoholic) as well as snacks. For me, I have taken a liking to some great non-alcoholic beers and I make sure to have them on board. The difference is it is not a deal breaker if I DON'T have any onboard. I can take it or leave it. Also, I usually might have 2-3 all afternoon as I am no longer chasing a buzz. I'd rather not uselessly keep filling up my bladder. As far as concerts or sporting events, the same thing applies. Maybe one or two non alcoholic beers but maybe not too. I am happy not to spend $15 for each cheap wine or can of Bud Light (eww). The concession stands at concerts and ballgames are absolutely out to screw you with their overpriced drinks. Don't miss that at all. And also don't miss all the time I missed the event because I was standing in line for the drink or in the men's room, relieving myself.

POST: So I've been sober for 6 days, I drank because I thought it would help me manage my crappy life. Now that I haven't drunk I realize my life actually is crap. I'm a full time caregiver for my husband, a person I don't like or love, and was going to leave a number of years ago when he became ill so I stayed.

I'm just wondering how people cope whose lives are crappier sober because they now have to face the questions of making their lives happier.

ME: When you continually take an anesthetic daily to dull the pain of life it is no surprise that a happy and fulfilling life would elude you. And alcoholism is a very selfish disease. It is hard to care for people (especially care for them in the right way) when you are in the throes of addiction. For many people it is easier to remain chained to the bonds of their addiction rather than face the underlying cause/s of the addiction. To begin your sober journey, the first step is simply NOT to take the poison into your mouth. But to maintain sobriety, the addict must uncover the real psychological reasons for the addiction in the first place. Once identified, the issues must be addressed (with professional help if necessary), or the time sober will more than likely be unfortunately fleeting. The person in the post above seems to be caught in a no win situation where she is putting her ill husband ahead of her own needs. In reality, I would think it doubtful that she has no time for herself at all. Get the husband's need set then possibly a workout routine, online, course, write a book, etc. Getting sober and remaining that way is all about filling up your time with new and positive endeavors.

A Recent Visit by Friends Involving Excessive Alcohol Consumption (Insanity Exemplified) and Some Other Observations

Just last night (as I write this) we had friends of the family over for dinner. One of the guests we have known for over 20 years and I know him to be an absolute lush. Every time I see him he gets "fall down" drunk. Last night was no exception as he ended up falling down the stairs on the way out. I watched him go from a few scotches neat to a chocolate martini. Then he wanted beer. We were out of beer and I told him this but of course he couldn't hear me in his now semi comatose state. My wife, out of habit, went down to my beer kegerator which is in my garage and is now unplugged and has been for about 6 months. It still has some old beer in it (unrefrigerated) that has been sitting in there. She gets him a glass and brings it to him. I tell him it's no good and explain. He puts ice in the beer and drinks it down anyway and gives me a thumbs up that it tastes good!

How could this possibly taste good? How can it not taste anything but horrible? But for him, just to keep the fuel flowing through his veins it would suffice. The need to relieve the stress caused by yesterday's drinking and to chase that blissful state that no longer seems to be achievable, no matter how many drinks consumed. This is the endless loop. So as I sit here writing this morning - happy, clear headed, and productive I wonder what our friend is feeling now. His is a life that has fallen well short of any potential he was ever given. He is later middle age, with no wife, no kids, no career, no home, no car, a bad gambling habit and drinking to excess everyday. Alcohol will steal it all over time.

I have some friends of mine where the wife is always drunk every time I have been in their company. I mean EVERY time. They are Facebook friends and have just finished up a beautiful 2 week Mediterranean cruise. I enjoy seeing the pictures of all the beautiful places they are visiting. It is great to see them having so much fun together and it is great that they can share this experience with friends via social media. True to her form, however, every set of pictures has at least the wife but most of the time both of them consuming alcohol. They have made it a point to visit a lot of wineries and taste the different wines on the visits. This would probably be a great experience for many couples and indeed worthwhile excursions for many. However, I know the importance of alcohol in the life of the wife. Nothing else could be more important than alcohol, and every day all day, especially on vacation. I have seen her passed out drunk many times and never without a drink in hand in social settings and always a picture of booze in Facebook posts. It reminds me of myself in my earlier life. I didn't even realize that alcohol was ALWAYS my goal, it was the way I recreated and nothing was as fun as it could be without it. Go to a brewery or winery? I'm in. Go visit my sick great aunt on a Sunday afternoon in the hospital (zero alcohol). Not today, we'll go another time.

Just the other day (as I write this passage), I took a young business associate out on my boat with his girlfriend and several of their friends who were visiting the Atlantic City area on a beautiful summer day. We had a great time on the boat and they were all enjoying themselves drinking the White Claw I provided in my cooler while I nursed my Coors Edge (non alcoholic beer). Mind you these kids could easily be MY kids as they are in their 20's. They were so excited to be going out that night to a club. with pre club cocktails at a friend's house. It took me back in my mind to my youth. Will this just be a passing phase for them until they get married, have kids and grow up? Or will they be like me and millions of others who were once in their shoes but stuck with it and crossed the line to problem drinking? Or will they go even further and lose it all, like Ralph or my Dad?

My Typical Loop of Drinking

This is how I rolled and is probably pretty common for many problem drinkers.

In my mind, one drink has never been worth it. Why bother?! Two drinks, I start to feel all warm and fuzzy, so I go for the third to keep that feeling going! The third drink is about when I may call an old friend or family member to chat or maybe start a movie. But, while I am chatting and/or watching the movie I pour myself a fourth drink because I have squarely reached my comfort zone. I am drinking this drink to keep this feeling going, I am feeling really good and my mood is high. If there is still time on the clock - because of course I have to go to bed at 11pm so I can function the next day - I might even have a nightcap at this point. This is the point that I can never really recall the next day as I have probably consumed enough for my brain to shut down. Blackout drunk, it just sort of creeped up on me yet again. From here I somehow get myself together enough to walk upstairs and pass out in bed. Then, I wake up at 3am. What did I say? Do? Binge eat? I am again overcome with anxiety and fear. Did the person I was talking to know how drunk I was? What in the world did I say? My goodness, I can't remember what I watched let alone remember the story. Then, I somehow manage to gradually get back to a very unrestful sleep until 6 am. I wake up and expend a great deal of energy just to make it through my day. Then, around 5pm I think....I'll just have one glass of wine...

And THAT is why I quit drinking!

Now I personally didn't drink to this excess every night but I sure did many times. But one thing is clear to me now - I always drank when I was bored. And I was bored a lot. My drinking hobby was great at filling up my calendar with things to do. Lunches, dinners, brunches, happy hours, football games on tv, family parties. So now living sober, it is important to establish new ways to fill up this time. To be honest it is not always easy and sometimes I end up wracking my brain thinking of something to do that does not involve taking a drink. Because taking a drink would be so easy. I could go to any bar, order a drink, strike up a conversation with a stranger next to me, get a buzz and be there for a few hours. But I won't do that now. It is not worth the price no matter how bored I am. I will not piss away my hard earned money on overpriced alcohol any more. I will not wake up with poison running through my veins. I will not go to work with a pounding headache. I will not wake up at 4 am wide awake with stimulants created by a brain fighting the effects of alcohol and not able to fall back asleep (leading to being exhausted the next day). I will not create an artificial stress that can only be relieved by taking another drink and the cycle repeating endlessly, day in/day out, week in/week out, year in/year out. Here is a short list of activities I will do now instead of taking the easy way out and going to a bar:

1) Walking. Probably my favorite activity. I am fortunate to have several world renowned seaside boardwalks very close to my home and a short drive away. We also are not far from some great walking trails. My wife also enjoys walking, so this is a double bonus to get exercise and spend time together.
2) Boating. I love all things having to do with the water. My boat is a short drive away and I text the marina when I want to go in for the day (I have in/out rack service). Great for spending time with others or just to get out by myself for a couple of hours
3) Biking. I enjoy taking out my road bike from time to time to get some fresh air, see the sights and get the blood pumping

4) Go to my cigar club and puff on a cigar and talk to my buddies. Even though it is a tobacco product and not free of its own set of health risks- I smoke (don't inhale) a cigar pretty much daily. I have a group of friends at my club and I know I can always strike up a conversation and relax with a stogie when I go here.
5) Go to my community pool (summer months). I can go here by myself or with my son to pass a couple hours and swim, read a book or socialize. I used to sneak large amounts of vodka into the pool area and get hammered for the afternoon with no one the wiser. How pathetic, I see others doing the same now. I know the mindset.
6) Play ball with my son. Kick a soccer ball or have a catch. It is good, clean and simple fun but we both tire of it quickly.
7) Work. I am self employed in real estate/mortgages. I have a seemingly unending to-do list for marketing these endeavors. I can work wherever and whenever I choose thanks to the marvels of modern technology. I do enjoy my work and should probably do more of it.
8) Chauffeur my son to his activities. I would be happy for our 4th grade son to be involved with a couple of extracurricular activities outside of school. However my wife (an asian "tiger mom") sees it fit for him to have no less than 7 activities going on during the week. We are constantly running him from one activity to the next. I used to complain but now I realize that it is good for him (as long as we are not wearing him out, he is enjoying it, and it is not interfering with his school work) and also good for me to stay on task. Because I know where boredom can lead...

9) Go to my local Starbucks. I started going here last year and would go in after dropping my son off to school. This year he has the bus and I no longer have to go here but I go anyway to talk to my friends and get my morning coffee fix. I try to limit my caffeinated coffee to one large but have 2-3 decafs as well. Coffee is a large part of my daily fluid intake. But my hour here is better than an hour in the bar. I am in control of the time and money I spend here, not so much at the bar.

Do you need to go to AA?

Different things will work for different people. The AA philosophy is centered around the concept that you are a broken, diseased person who can never enjoy the thing in this world you most love-alcohol. You must admit your failings for the rest of your life and always consider yourself a hopeless alcoholic. You must take "one day at a time" and avoid your beloved drinking even if it means sheltering yourself from activities and people you love. This is a hard road for most people. Many people also have an issue with the "higher power" concept as well. You must surrender yourself to God or a "Higher Power". This doesn't work well for atheists. With all this considered, no wonder AA has an approximately 92% failure rate! However, it has also helped millions of people conquer their addiction and has saved countless lives. It works well for many and doesn't work for others. Thankfully, today there are other ways for people to get sober.

Regarding AA, here is a snippet from a great article on the topic published in the Los Angeles Times on March 3, 2011 right at the time when idiot Charlie Sheen was making the news due to his buffoonery:

Charlie Sheen claims AA has a 5% success rate -- is he right?

BY JEANNINE STEIN, LOS ANGELES TIMES, AND MARY FORGIONE, TRIBUNE HEALTH

MARCH 3, 2011 12 AM PT

Actor Charlie Sheen's recent rambling rants included several tirades against the 12-step program popularized by Alcoholics Anonymous: He called it a "bootleg cult" and claimed it had only a 5% success rate.

While we're not believing much of what Sheen is spouting, that 5% statistic has people talking. Does the massively popular program really do that bad a job at combating alcohol abuse?

AA stats are hard to come by, since the organization doesn't conduct studies on itself. A 2007 membership survey reported that 33% of members said they'd been consistently sober for more than 10 years, 12% were sober for five to 10 years, 24% were sober for one to five years, and 31% were sober for less than one year. However, the numbers don't reveal the total number of years the members have been in the program.

Addiction specialists cite numbers closer to 8% to 12% for sobriety by members after the first year. Even Dr. Drew Pinsky of "Celebrity Rehab" acknowledged that Sheen's statement had some cred. "He's got a point," Pinsky said to TMZ recently. "Their success rates aren't that great. But the fact is, it does work when people do it."

A Cochrane Review that combined studies looking at AA and other 12-step programs found 12-step programs weren't any more effective in decreasing alcohol abuse compared with other treatments, although researchers found limitations with some of the studies.

The article continues with some additional pluses and minuses regarding AA.

Fortunately, we live in an age where technology, as much as it can be a major productivity waster, is also great for learning how to live alcohol free. I will review the resources I have found in my recap below in the conclusion. It would be wise for those seeking to rid themselves of this poison to learn to embrace whatever method will help change their own mindsets. Whether it be a formal group meeting concept like AA, YouTube videos, quit lit books, or anything else.

Non Alcoholic Beer, Wine and Spirits

Non alcoholic drinks are gaining traction in today's marketplace now more than ever. To drink them or not is an interesting subject and slightly controversial in the quit lit I've read and Facebook Groups I belong to. Is it ok to drink non-alcoholic versions of beer, wine and now even spirits? My answer is YES, well sort of...

For non alcoholic beer or "near beer", one should be cautioned that many of these beers are marketed with a label that says they contain less than .5% alcohol. The normal alcohol range for beer is about 5% but can be as high as 14%:

Beer brand	Alcohol percentage
Bud Light	4.2%
Guinness	4.27%
Coors Light	4.2%
Budweiser	5%
Carlsburg	5%
Peroni	5.1%
Corona	4.8%
Moretti	4.6%

So there is SOME alcohol present in most NA beers. For me, it is negligible and I find that I can have one or two with no problem. I don't feel the need to drink any more than that, in the same way I wouldn't want to consume more than one or two of any other drink like iced tea or club soda. It is hard to fathom that some drinkers will go to a bar or pub and drink 5-6 pints of beer with no problem, but drinking that much water or soda in one sitting is absolutely ludicrous.

I enjoy Heineken 0 and am also a big fan of Brewdog Punk AF. Both are relatively low in calories and carbs as well. As far as non-alcoholic wine, I think it is ok, but not really worth the price as it costs almost the same as regular wine and I really don't care for the taste anyway. I prefer a spritzer of seltzer water with some fruit juice added. A relatively new concept is non alcoholic spirits, which are really expensive and in my opinion don't really offer any benefit at all.

One needs to be careful with the reasons WHY you are drinking non alcoholic drinks. Personally, I like the taste of some NA beers and do not find them to be a trigger to my drinking. It can also be sort of a "decoy" at a party when you have a beer bottle in your hand, cutting down on the questions of why you are not drinking. And if you're like me, you like to have something in your hand while socializing for some reason. Again, proceed with caution and make sure you are mindful of what you are doing. If it is a trigger for you, these are products to avoid.

Conclusion

At the time of writing, I am coming up on a year AF. It should be more like 4 years but I attempted to "moderate" twice and failed and went back into full problem drinking mode both times. I am now off ALL medications that I was on for years that were just treating the symptoms brought on by excessive drinking and a poor diet that it often brings with it - for me, namely high blood pressure, anxiety, high cholesterol. My A1C (the simple blood test that measures your average blood sugar levels over the past 3 months) was in the beginning stage of DIABETIC at 6.7 six months ago and today it is NORMAL at 5.5. My weight is down roughly 40 pounds year to date.

I have read both of William Porter's excellent books and also listen to Craig Beck's (Stop Drinking Expert) YouTube posts all the time. Both are great resources and there are also some Facebook groups that I belong to and read and contribute to everyday. One is "Be Sober - Quit Drinking & Enjoy Life" and the other is "Alcohol Explained". Annie Grace "The Naked Mind" and Kevin O'Hara "Habits Unplugged" YouTube videos are excellent resources as well and have helped and continue to help me on my journey. All have helped me turn my life around and rid myself of the drug once and for all.

I see so many people's posts of counting days, trying to make it through one day at a time, having bad craving days, etc. Basically having a hard time giving up drinking. That was me before also, and in a way still is. But I think when you really make peace with this is when you really see the drug for what it is and genuinely don't want it back in your life. You realize that there are NO benefits at all. You see through the illusion. You realize that your memories of the "good times" drinking are never coming back. Those memories involve a different person that I no longer desire to be because life has so much more to offer. I have learned to stop chasing those memories and now embrace my new sober memories. And boy do I love my sober mornings especially!

The poison is becoming a smaller and smaller part of my life. Actually it would almost be non-existent except I want to do more to help others who were in the same rut as I was. So I do think about it a lot, but I think about the subject, not about wishing I could drink again. I do not envy the "old" me nor the people in my life I see that have the same habits. I thought it would be easier to share my story with others but I am actually finding it to be a bit of a challenge. It seems that I am close to so many people who are in the exact same situation I was in. So for me to pontificate to others about my newfound clean lifestyle would come off as hypocritical and drive a wedge into our relationship. It was not long ago that I was a problem drinker and had been for so long, so I have to be careful with how I tell my story to people I know personally. The best thing to do is to set an example and live by it.

My advice about the poison is don't make it any bigger than it has to be and focus on how much better life will be without it. Love your sobriety and make a big deal about it. Because life is truly better without it! Good luck my friends. Stay sober, get healthy and maybe even lose a few pounds. Feel free to email me at any time at johnepifanio@comcast.net. I would be happy to hear from you and would love to hear about your journey. Thanks for reading my book. It is my sincere desire that it will help others "finally wake up".

ABOUT THE AUTHOR

John Epifanio

John Epifanio is living his best (and sober) life these days just outside of Atlantic City, NJ with his wife and son. A graduate of Temple University (BBA '89), John ran two successful music stores for 22 years before moving on to the Real Estate and Mortgage industry full time. In addition to writing books, John enjoys boating, golf, scuba diving, language learning (currently Mandarin), cigars and music (when not running his son to all his activities).

Made in the USA
Middletown, DE
14 November 2022